SERMON OUTLINES

on

The Old Testament

Charles R. Wood

kregel
PUBLICATIONS

Grand Rapids, MI 49501

Sermon Outlines on The Old Testament

Copyright © 1999 by Charles R. Wood.

Published in by Kregel Publications, a division of Kregel, Inc., P.O. Box 2607, Grand Rapids, MI 49501. Kregel Publications provides trusted, biblical publications for Christian growth and service. Your comments and suggestions are valued.

Library of Congress Cataloging-in-Publication Data
Wood, Charles R. (Charles Robert), 1933–
    Sermon outlines on the Old Testament / Charles R. Wood.
        p.   cm. (Easy-to-use sermon outline series)
    Includes index.
    1. Bible. O.T. Sermons—Outlines, syllabi, etc. I. Title.
II. Series: Wood, Charles R. (Charles Robert), 1933– Easy-to-use sermon outline series.
BV1151.5.W66   1999   251'.02—dc21   98-50468
                                                    CIP

ISBN 0-8254-4139-0

2 3 4 5 6 / 07 06 05 04 03

Printed in the United States of America

Contents

Introduction

The Old Testament is a veritable spiritual gold mine. It is filled with doctrinal truth, illustrative stories, fascinating narrative, practical admonition, and a host of other valuable verities. Preaching from the Old Testament is to dig into treasures of incomparable wealth.

The compiler of this book of outlines first fell in love with Old Testament preaching as the result of emphases during seminary days, and he has continued to preach from that wonderful portion of the sacred text for more than forty years. We frequently say that the Bible is inexhaustible as a source for preaching. This is certainly true, but the Old Testament in itself possesses that same characteristic.

The sermons that are included in this book cover a fairly wide range of Old Testament passages and themes. They have been selected, however, with an eye to the practical teaching set forth in the passages selected. If the Bible is a book of principles to be lived rather than a book of facts to be known, then these outlines will provide assistance in making the Word come alive in life.

As is always true of sermon outline books, the greatest possible benefit—both to the preacher and his preaching—will be derived if a period of time is set aside for the study of the text, the consideration of the subject addressed, and the consideration of a basic Bible commentary. These outlines are designed, in most instances, to be suggestive rather than exhaustive. They may easily be expanded on by a thoughtful, creative preacher. In some instances it is likely that more than one sermon might arise out of a single outline.

All of the outlines included in this volume have been preached by the compiler of this book within the last four or five years. They definitely will "preach," as they have had demonstrable impact on a specific congregation.

These outlines are sent forth with the sincere hope that they might prove useful to many servants of God. It is the prayer of the compiler that they will be springboards for other ideas and approaches, and that they might make a contribution to the improvement of the pulpit work being done in many church settings. May God bless them to that end!

CHARLES R. WOOD

The Hazards of the Horizontal

Genesis 34–37

Introduction:

In some ways it is good to be "laid-back." There is a danger, however, in being too laid-back. Jacob had a family disaster because he was too laid-back.

I. The Incident with Dinah (34:1–2)
   A. Jacob lived among the heathen
   B. Dinah went to some specific heathen function
   C. She was defiled by one of the princes of the land
   D. Jacob appears to have been careless regarding her safety

II. The Avenging of Dinah's Rape (34:5, 13, 30)
   A. The heathen seek to act somewhat honorably
   B. Jacob allows his sons to respond for him (vv. 5, 13)
   C. His sons act deceitfully (two slew, the rest spoiled)
   D. Vengeance is exacted from all for the act of one
   E. Jacob does nothing but issue a mild rebuke, and he rebukes them for the effect of their action on him rather than for the evil of what they had done

III. The Sin of Reuben (35:22)
   A. He had relations with his father's concubine
      1. A concubine was viewed as the same as a wife
      2. This "in your face" act involved specific rebellion
   B. Jacob knew about this and did nothing about it

IV. The Strife Among His Children (37:2–3, 11, 13–14)
   A. The strife was intensified by Jacob's behavior
      1. "Coat of many colors," a symbol of privilege
      2. Jacob's favoritism engendered resentment
   B. Joseph's foolish act of boasting stands unrebuked
   C. Jacob had to know of the brothers' hatred of Joseph
   D. Jacob sent him to his brothers regardless, leaving him outside his protection
   E. For all intents and purposes, Joseph was murdered

Conclusion:

Jacob was extremely clever and successful in commerce but casual and laid-back in relation to his family. The message for us: Fathers—What's going on in your family? What do you know you need to deal with but aren't? Parents—What are you tolerating although it grieves you? Individuals—What needs to be dealt with, but you are allowing to slide by?

A Rock and a Hard Place

Exodus 14

Introduction:

Israel was between a rock and a hard place immediately after leaving Egypt. We face some of the same situations with no apparent way out. The story of Israel provides us with important principles in our times of great difficulty.

I. **Difficulties Are Indicative of Nothing**
    A. Israel went as God directed
        1. They were in difficult straits
        2. They were in the will of God
    B. Our difficulties—and those of others—prove exactly nothing
        1. Sometimes they are of our own making
        2. Often they are of God's direction and allowance

II. **There Is an Overriding Providence in Difficulties**
    A. God was working out His purposes on Pharaoh
        1. Pharaoh assumed that the Israelites were trapped
        2. He saw his opportunity for revenge
    B. Most of this whole matter was not designed for Israel—they were mere bystanders!
        1. They were being used of God to accomplish His purposes
        2. Those purposes would have benefit for them as well
    C. Just as no man stands alone, no trial comes alone
        1. Our lives are part of a greater providence that is being worked out
        2. Our self-centeredness keeps us from seeing what God is doing through us

III. **There Is a Personal Purpose in Difficulties**
    A. God had His reasons with Israel
        1. He knew what they were going to face
        2. He wanted to provide them a "sample" of His miraculous power
        3. He wanted to remove a powerful enemy from them
        4. He wanted to arm them for coming battles
        5. The whole matter was instructive and preparatory, not punitive
    B. If they had not been brought here, they could not have seen a double miracle

   1. They were delivered, and Egypt was destroyed

   2. Both were accomplished in one basic act

IV. Reactions to Difficulties Are Very Important

  A. What their reaction should have been

   1. "Fear ye not"

   2. "Stand still"—be calm, composed, in control

   3. "See the salvation of the Lord"—watch, observe, learn

   4. "The Lord will fight for us"—trust

   5. "Ye shall hold your peace"—stop complaining

  B. What it actually was

   1. They got angry with God ("as the Egyptians were angry with themselves for the best deed they ever did, so Israel was angry with God for the best favor ever done them")

   2. They got angry with Moses ("the leader is always a convenient target for the frustrations of followers")

   3. They said some incredible things ("Give me life or give me bondage" rather than "Give me liberty or give me death")

   4. They established bad patterns for later difficulties

  C. What it teaches us

   1. Our reactions in difficulties usually don't determine where we will come out, they just determine whether or not we will benefit from the experience

   2. "God brings us into straits so He can bring us to our knees"

Conclusion:

  Moses shows us how to handle "rock and hard place" situations. He turned to the Lord. "Moses' silent [unrecorded] prayer of faith prevailed more with God than Israel's loud outcries of fear."

Love Thy Neighbor

Leviticus 19:9–18

Introduction:

Jesus said, "Thou shalt love the Lord thy God with all thy heart, soul, and mind. This is the first commandment. The second is like it, thou shalt love thy neighbor as thyself." But how can I love my neighbor? According to this passage, I can love my neighbors by:

I. **Making Provision for Their Needs (vv. 9–10)**
   A. This involves a mind-set, a way of thinking
   B. Note that there is no command to give, just one to provide

II. **Practicing Integrity in All My Relationships (v. 11)**
   A. This rules out such things as lying, cheating, and stealing
   B. Any lack of integrity equals a lack of love—treating others this way shows lack of love for them

III. **Refraining from Invoking God's Name (v. 12)**
   A. There is more involved here than merely taking God's name in vain
   B. This involves invoking the will of God on someone
      1. It involves such things as "the Lord told me"
      2. It is using God's name or will in any way that justifies harm to another person

IV. **Keeping My Commitments (v. 13)**
   A. I must treat my neighbor justly and equitably
   B. I will pay a fair wage and do it promptly
   C. No one can grow rich at the expense of another and claim to love that person

V. **Caring for Neighbors Who Are Less Fortunate Than I (v. 14)**
   A. This has to do with proper assistance and provision for the handicapped
   B. It can be extended to not making fun of anyone's discomfiture

VI. **Treating My Neighbors As Equal to Me and to All Others (v. 15)**
   A. All people are to be viewed as having equal worth
   B. Note carefully that it says neither rich nor poor are to be preferred just because they are rich or poor

VII. Speaking Truthfully (v. 16)
  A. Love is truthful, but it seeks to focus on the good
  B. Love never needlessly brings harm to a neighbor
  C. This rules out any form of character assassination

VIII. Rejecting Hateful Thoughts (v. 17a)
  A. Hatred is the opposite of love
  B. Thinking hateful thoughts is dangerous as it can result in hateful actions (one rarely does what one has not first thought of doing)

IX. Rebuking My Neighbor When He or She Is Wrong (v. 17b)
  A. This is a forgotten aspect of love—love rebukes when it sees wrong
  B. The purpose of this rebuke is to keep individuals from suffering for their sins
  C. Such rebuke would be easier to deliver if God's people were more open to receiving it

X. Refusing to Entertain Wrong Desires (v. 18)
  A. This deals with grudges and thoughts of revenge
  B. Love rules out even wrong desires for another's ill-being; rejoicing in another's misfortune is a violation of love

Conclusion:
"Ministry takes place when divine resources meet human needs through loving channels to the glory of God."—Warren Wiersbe

The Choice Is Yours

Deuteronomy 30:19; Joshua 24:15

Introduction:

We are constantly faced with choices, and there would be even more except that many practices have been moved into the realm of habit. Even when we feel trapped in life, we have a vast range of choice. Many freedoms have been taken from us; choice is the last bastion of freedom.

I.   **The Situation of Choice**
   A.   God allows us enormous freedom
      1.   It is within the scope of His sovereignty
      2.   The scope of that freedom is readily observable
   B.   That freedom necessarily involves choice
      1.   We can usually do things several ways
      2.   We actually only have two ways spiritually—His way or our way
   C.   The Bible continually calls on us to make right choices

II.   **The Scope of Choice—I Choose**
   A.   What I think about
   B.   The ways in which I generally think
   C.   Indirectly, how I feel
   D.   What I say or don't say
   E.   What I do; what actions I take
   F.   What I don't do; the actions I refrain from taking
   G.   How I respond or react to people and circumstances
   H.   What kind of person I am becoming

III.   **The Significance of Choice**
   Premise: I actually choose what I think, say, and do, thus:
   A.   I am responsible for what I think, say, and do
      1.   This lays a heavy weight of responsibility on me
      2.   This is a most liberating concept—I am not a helpless victim
   B.   My habits represent a cluster of my repeated choices
      1.   I choose to do many things the same way every time
      2.   Those choices harden into habits
      3.   Bad habits can be broken; good habits can be established, but it is done by conscious choices
   C.   My choices always have results and consequences
      1.   Positive results flow from my choices
      2.   Negative consequences flow from my choices

3. I'm not always able to distinguish how my choices will come out
4. This is why it is important to do right regardless—this is the only way one can be sure of results rather than consequences

D. My choices are worthy of much more consideration than I usually give them
   1. There are many more small than large choices
   2. Most large choices, however, are the outgrowth of many smaller choices
   3. Most choices I make have significance

Conclusion:

This is an enormous responsibility as there is incredible freedom in choice. Satan works to keep us from making right choices. We must seek God's daily guidance for all choices and His specific help in the particular ones that stand out.

In Tough Times

Joshua 1:2–9

Introduction:

"Moses my servant is dead; now . . ." This was a great turning point in the experience of God's people. They were facing a time of transition but also a challenging adventure.

I.   **The Challenge: So much lay before them**
     A.   The challenge of change
          1.   In leadership—from Moses to Joshua
          2.   In status—from nomad to settled
          3.   In activity—from peaceful to warlike
     B.   The challenge of crossing
          1.   They had been through this before, but it was more daunting now as the water was at flood stage and there was an enemy on the other side
          2.   There was almost no one there with any personal experience
     C.   The challenge of conquest
          1.   The nations were entrenched
          2.   The nations were experienced in battle
          3.   The nations were fighting for their homelands
     D.   The challenge of control
          1.   They were undisciplined wanderers
          2.   They had a "manna mentality"
          3.   They had tried this before, and it didn't work
          4.   They had a bad inheritance background
     E.   The challenge of closure
          1.   He was to divide (assign) the inheritance
          2.   There were boundaries, but they never got to them

II. **The Commandment (vv. 6–7, 9)**
     A.   It was stated: Be strong and of good courage
     B.   It was repeated for emphasis and because of need
     C.   It was defined "Don't be afraid" and "Don't be dismayed"—which implies a call for persistence

III. **The Certainties (vv. 5, 9)**
     A.   Be sure of my presence—"as I was with Moses"
     B.   Be sure of my power—"I am able to do whatever I need to do" and "I will do what I have said I will do"
     C.   Be sure of my promise—"No one will be able to withstand you until you complete the task for which I send you"

D. Be sure of my provision—"I have given you my word"
E. Be sure of my purpose—"I will have you possess the land"

Conclusion:

God gave Joshua a tough challenge, but God gave Joshua what he needed to accomplish the task. You may be facing a tough challenge in your life. God will give you what you need to accomplish it—just be sure you are faithful to His Word.

The Sin of Achan

Joshua 7

Introduction:

We seldom deal with the actual sin of Achan but rather with the consequences of his sin. What did Achan do that got him killed? Let's look at the story.

I.   **The Story of Achan**
  A. The background
    1. Israel was before Jericho
    2. God gave them directions about the conquest
    3. God gave them orders regarding their conduct in conquest
  B. The sequel
    1. They next moved on to Ai
    2. They were defeated there by a small force
    3. This caused great grief and consternation
  C. The judgment
    1. Joshua was told by God that the defeat was the result of sin
    2. Directions were given him for ferreting out the problem
    3. Achan and probably all his family were killed by the judgment

II. **The Sin of Achan**
  A. What did Achan do?
    1. He took something that wasn't his
    2. He took something that was forbidden
    3. He took something that belonged to God (6:17–19)
  B. What is the lesson of the sin of Achan?
    1. It is not primarily the problem of "sin in the camp"
    2. It is actually about the cost of taking for one's self that which belongs to God

III. **The Lesson of Achan**
  A. It is dangerous to take that which belongs to God
    1. The penalty is certainly not always death, but there is always a price
    2. We need to be aware of what belongs to God
  B. What are some things that belong to God?
    1. Interpretations (especially of dreams, etc.)—the price of taking them is false prophecies (Gen. 40:8)

2. Secret things—the price of taking them is confusion (Deut. 29:29)
3. Vengeance and recompense—the price of taking them is that God stops dealing with the issue (Deut. 32:35; Rom. 12:19; Prov. 24:17–18)
4. Issues of life and death—we are seeing what intervening with this does in the abortion and euthanasia mess (Ps. 68:20)
5. The tithe—the principle was established in Genesis; it was regulated by the law but assumed by men; it forms the basis for giving in all times; failure to tithe (or at least to give) is thus viewed as taking something that belongs to God (Lev. 27:30; Mal. 3:8–10)
6. Salvation—God has determined the method of salvation, and it is through the finished work of Christ alone (Rev. 19:9)
   a. To teach any other way of salvation is to take something that belongs to God
   b. The price of doing so is eternal damnation

Conclusion:
Achan took something that belonged to God, and he paid the ultimate price for that. There are a number of things that belong to God, and we always pay a price when we take one of them.

The Success of a Senior Saint

Joshua 14:5–15

Introduction:

One of the laws of thermodynamics says that things left to themselves tend to run down. This is true in life in general as we tend to grow tired and slack off as life goes on. This law works in the spiritual realm as well. We lose the first glow of salvation, we become easily discouraged, we gradually stop doing things that we should do, and our Christianity tends to run out of steam. Caleb was the exception.

I. Caleb Had Been Around a Long Time
A. Retrace the story of the spies
   1. They were sent on a specific mission—they were to find out what the land was like and how best to approach its conquest
   2. They did something they were not asked to do—they evaluated possibilities
   3. Caleb and Joshua stuck to the original task
B. Caleb was required to wait
   1. He was held back by the negativity of others
   2. He was forced to endure something that was not his fault
C. Caleb watched a long history develop
   1. He was born at least forty years before his time
   2. He kept hope aflame while others burned out

II. Caleb Did Not Lose His Enthusiasm
A. Caleb desired all that God had for him
   1. He saw his life incomplete until this was achieved
   2. He understood his task and was faithful to it
B. Caleb was willing to pay a price for what God had promised him
   1. He was well aware of the difficulty of the task as he had spied out this portion of the land
   2. He was totally confident of His ability as aided by God
C. Caleb retained his vigor and determination
   1. His age was a factor, but he overcame it
   2. He did accomplish what he set out to do

III. **Caleb Had a Reason for Staying Fresh: He wholly followed the Lord**
   A. It was not a matter of mysticism
   B. His life was squarely based on God's word—he keeps quoting God, and he obviously believed what God had said (vv. 5, 10, 12—"the Lord said")
   C. Notice the signs of his belief in God's Word
      1. He believed the promises enough to wait for them
      2. He believed in God enough to obey the commandments
   D. Notice the benefits of belief in God's Word
      1. It keeps one above the flow of circumstances
      2. It gives marching orders from heaven, not from one's surroundings
   E. Notice the results of belief in God's Word:
      1. Attention to duty
      2. Attempts to be like Christ
      3. Dedication to one's task

Conclusion:

We tend to run down in our Christian lives, and we stop doing things and don't replace them with others. The longer we go, the colder we become. The problem lies in not wholly following the Lord. Somewhere we get away from the Word, and when we get away from that tie to the Word, we slip. Don't run out of gas on the way to church!

How Art the Mighty Fallen!

1 Kings 11:1–8

Introduction:

Christians sometimes do incredible things and fall incredible distances. What happens? How can it be? What goes wrong? Who can fall? An analysis of the life of Solomon can provide us with cautions.

I. **Solomon on Top: He was a botanist, zoologist, architect, poet, historian, philosopher, scholar, statesman, diplomat, patron of the arts, etc.**
    A. He had an incredible background—he had seen enough to keep him straight
    B. He had a widespread kingdom—he took over in Israel at its all-time prime
    C. He made a splendid request—he asked for wisdom to rule rather than for personal gain
    D. He received profound wisdom—he was the wisest man in world of his time
    E. He possessed great wealth—it was actually given to him because he didn't seek it, and with it, he became an object of wonder in the world
    F. He had largeness of heart (4:29)
    G. He was the builder of a magnificent edifice
    H. He was the preacher of a splendid sermon (8:12–21)
    I. He was the prayer of a marvelous prayer (8:22–53)
    J. He was the writer of incredible books
    K. He was the practitioner of intelligent diplomacy
    L. He was the possessor of direct revelation (3:5; 9:2; with 11:9)

II. **Solomon at Bottom: The distance between the top and the bottom was probably never greater for any man who ever lived**
    A. He had strange women—some of them were the result of alliances with other countries
    B. He had a huge harem—it was likely more political than sensual
    C. He knew harassment
        1. He had known outward peace
        2. Now Hadad, Rezin, and Jereboam gave him trouble
    D. He turned away from the Lord
        1. His heart was not perfect with the Lord (11:4)

        2. He went after other gods (at least he tolerated them, seduced by his multiple wives)
   E. He lost most of what he had been given
        1. His kingdom was lost after his death, but he knew before he died that it would be
        2. Everything fell apart within weeks of his death
   F. He produced a foolish, self-willed son

III. Solomon's Digression: Solomon didn't fall overnight—it was a process that went on throughout his reign, and it was caused by
   A. Complacency—the worst things only showed up when he was older (v. 6 or so)
   B. Arrogance—he was very sure that he would not, could not fall
   C. An undisciplined thought life
        1. This is indicated in Ecclesiastes
        2. There is danger not only in what we think but in how we think
   D. The seduction by Satan—the appeal of the flesh
   E. The tendency to softness—he liked his leisure and leisure is always a danger
   F. A measure of halfheartedness
        1. He wasn't fully committed to what he did
        2. He did things for reasons other than love for the Lord
   G. The adoption of foreign deities—we have picked up the gods of the world around us, and we tend to become like what we worship
   H. Outright disobedience—to the Law in general and to specific commandments of God
   I. Incomplete commitment—halfway Christianity—He was likely a "political animal"
   J. Lack of repentance
        1. His writings show a great deal of sorrow, pain, etc.
        2. But no indication whatever of repentance

Conclusion:
We have all seen some frightening things in people's lives. We have found some explanations in Solomon's life. Anyone can fall! Falling is normally a process, the result of an accumulation of small actions and departures. Knowing better is absolutely no safeguard! Daily obedience to God's Word is the only sure safeguard. Sometimes we almost want to ask, "Who's next?" Don't let it be you!

Solomon on Sin

2 Chronicles 6:12–42

Introduction:

Solomon built a house for the Lord—he finished the job begun by his father David. Solomon was the wisest man in his world. It is helpful to look at the dedication of that house and to learn some things from it.

I. **Solomon Knew the Real Problem in the Realm of Religion**
   A. Note his repeated refrain
      1. It is not worship, praise, morality, improvement, expression of religious feelings, right conduct, etc.
      2. The recurring refrain is sin and forgiveness (vv. 21–22, 24–25, 26–27, 29–30, 36–39)
   B. The real core issue in religion is sin
      1. We are born in sin (Ps. 51:5)
      2. We are constantly committing sin
      3. We are separated from God by sin
      4. We are bearing a load of guilt because of sin

II. **Solomon Knew That Only God Can Forgive Sin**
   A. Modern man tries various ways to deal with sin
      1. Redefinition
      2. Denial
   B. It is impossible to deal adequately with sin without reference to God
      1. There is no adequate definition that way
      2. There is no satisfying solution
   C. Only God can forgive sin because
      1. All sin is ultimately sin against God
      2. Only the offended can truly forgive the offender

III. **Solomon Knew That God Desires to Forgive Sin**
   A. He prayed for forgiveness in anticipation of receiving it
      1. He mentions some serious sins, but he anticipates forgiveness
      2. He recognized that it is of the nature of God to forgive
   B. God has made provision for sin
      1. He sent His Son to die for it
      2. He has preserved the good news of what His Son did for posterity

C. God wants to forgive you
   1. Of sin as a principle by receiving what Christ did for you on the cross
   2. Of specific sin by confession—confession is agreement with God that it is sin—and by seeking forgiveness

Conclusion:

"All have sinned and come short of the glory of God." "If we confess our sin, He is faithful and just to forgive us our sin and to cleanse us from all iniquity." Have you dealt with the basic issue raised by Christianity?

Amaziah the Amazing

2 Chronicles 25

Introduction:

The story of the Hebrew kings is very complicated. This is at least partly true because their stories are recorded for us mainly where they are instructive for us. That explains our subject: Amaziah, son of Joash, king of Judah, a man with a good beginning and a tragic ending.

I. **Amaziah's Profile**
   A. His reign begins (vv. 1–4)
      1. He began his reign at 25 years of age
      2. He exacted justice for his father's death
      3. He followed the law regarding that justice
   B. His first war (vv. 5–12)
      1. It was against the Edomites
      2. He numbered the people and hired mercenaries
      3. He heeded the warning of the prophet
      4. He gained a great victory
   C. His second war (vv. 13–24)
      1. It was caused by disgruntled Israelites on a rampage
      2. Amaziah challenged Joash (Jehoash)
      3. There is a stunning defeat, and Amaziah is left in pillaged Jerusalem
   D. His life ends (vv. 25–28)
      1. We know little about the last years of his reign
      2. Ultimately he was the victim of a conspiracy

II. **Amaziah's Problem**
   A. There were flaws of character
      1. He lacked real confidence in God (vv. 5–6 with 8)
      2. He suffered from a measure of greed (v. 9)
      3. He had idolatry of heart—all idolatry is in the heart first (v. 14)
   B. There were follies of conduct
      1. He set up heathen gods—the gods of people he had just defeated (vv. 14–15)
      2. He refused to heed warnings (v. 16)
      3. He listened to ungodly counsel (v. 17)
   C. There were faults of attitude
      1. There was pride—pointed out by Jehoash, a wise man (v. 19)

2. There was conformity—He evidently did much because it was the thing to do
3. There was toleration (2 Kings 14:4)
D. This focuses the difficulty—he did what was right, but his heart was not really in it (v. 3)

III. Amaziah's Pointers
A. The danger of disobedience
  1. The first time the prophet comes, he heeds and is spared
  2. The second time, he disobeys and is destroyed
B. The challenge of circumstance
  1. The story is told because without it, we wouldn't know him
  2. Circumstances did nothing to Amaziah—they just revealed what he already was
C. The poison of pride
  1. He was evidently overwhelmed by his own success
  2. He didn't think he needed God's presence and help
D. The legacy of lunacy
  1. He acted exactly like his father (2 Kings 14:3)
  2. There are important issues here
    a. Kids will follow what you do and what you say
    b. They will either copy you and cause pain, or they will reject you and cause shame
E. The issue of the inner man
  1. Outward conformity catches up with us
  2. It is so crucial that the inner and the outer line up

Conclusion:
All of Amaziah's pointers boil down to one issue: the state of his heart. "He did right, but not with a perfect heart."

The Ministry of Opposition
Nehemiah 2:11–20

Introduction:
Satan is the busiest creature in the world, as he never rests, breaks down, or stops for any reason. What is Satan so busy doing? Opposing God! He fights God through every possible means. Nehemiah was committed to doing a job for God, within the will of God, and his experience is instructive.

I. **The Certainty of Opposition**
   A. As soon as Nehemiah began to move, trouble started
      1. Upon his arrival, there was trouble (v. 10)
      2. When the task was announced, there was more trouble (v. 19)
      3. Trouble continued to dog him until the task was completed
   B. Any step for God will result in opposition
      1. We should not be startled by it
      2. Opposition is no sign of being out of God's will
      3. No opposition? Are you "plugged in" with God?

II. **The Characteristics of Opposition**
   A. Its source (vv. 10–19):
      1. Some people:
         a. Sanballat—the governor of Samaria
         b. Tobiah—Sanballat's hired hand
         c. Geshem—Sanballat's hired gun
      2. Their relationship
         a. Sanballat was related to some Jews (6:18; 13:18)
         b. Tobiah is a Jewish name—was he a renegade Jew?
         c. These were people close to the Jews who should not have caused trouble—so much trouble comes to us from those who shouldn't be causing it
   B. Its form:
      1. Mockery—"laughed us to scorn"—ridicule—a familiar form
      2. Hatred—"despised"—demonstrated animosity
      3. False accusations—"Will ye rebel against the king?"
   C. Its motives:
      1. Selfishness—what the Jews got, these people didn't
      2. Jealousy—these people didn't want the Jews to get anything
      3. Simmering bitterness—these people had been

refused their own way in the long-ago past (Ezra 4:1–3)
   D. Some things never change
      1. The source of our opposition
      2. The form of our opposition
      3. The motives of our opposition

III. The Ministry of Opposition
   A. It caused Nehemiah to reevaluate
      1. His action was born in prayer (1:5–10; 2:4)
      2. His action was confirmed by providence (v. 18)
      3. His action had clearly been the will of God (v. 8)
   B. It caused Nehemiah to reaffirm
      1. He had called for dramatic action (v. 18)
      2. He had committed to that action ("us"; v. 18)
      3. He reaffirmed his intention to see that action through
   C. It caused Nehemiah to recommit (v. 20—"we . . . will arise and build")
      1. It made him more confident than ever
      2. It made him more determined than ever
      3. It made him more resolute (unwilling to quit)
   D. The ministry of opposition should make us:
      1. Reevaluate and be convinced God is in it
      2. Reaffirm our determination to go God's way
      3. Recommit and give ourselves anew to the task

IV. The Meeting of Opposition
   A. Nehemiah was very firm! He:
      1. Invoked God's role in the affair
      2. Publicly restated his determination to see it through
      3. Refused to yield a bit of ground
      4. Wouldn't honor his opponents
   B. Nehemiah thus provides us a pattern of what to do when opposition arises

Conclusion:

Have you begun something for God and the opposition has begun? Allow it to have a ministry in your life. Reevaluate what you are doing. Reaffirm the role of God in it. Recommit to sticking with the task no matter what.

That's No Way to Treat a Brother!

Nehemiah 5

Introduction:

Nehemiah had his hands full! He got the work well started, but external opposition arose to hinder it. He then got the work restarted, but people came to him with a bitter complaint.

I. **The Situation**
    A. There were three problems (vv. 1–5)
        1. People with large families did not have enough to eat
        2. They had mortgaged their homes and property to get food
        3. They were forced to sell their children to cover their debts
    B. Three causes
        1. Famine (v. 3)
        2. Taxes (v. 4)
        3. The sinful conduct of other Jews (v. 5)
    C. Nehemiah's response
        1. He became angry at these violations (v. 6)
        2. He confronted them with their sin—charging their brothers interest (v. 7); enslaving their own people (v. 8); and losing their distinctiveness before the heathen (v. 9)
        3. He condemned their sin (v. 10)
    D. Nehemiah's action
        1. He called for restoration (v. 11)
        2. He demanded an oath (v. 12)
        3. He invoked a curse for failure to keep that oath (v. 13)
    E. Nehemiah's example (vv. 14–19)

II. **The Sin**
    A. The biblical commandment
        1. It forbids the charging of interest (Exod. 22:25; Deut. 23:19–20)
        2. It forbids the taking advantage of poverty (Lev. 25:35–40)
    B. Their sinful actions
        1. What they were doing was sin
        2. They had obviously been doing it for a while
        3. They had lost concern for the teaching of the Word

C. The Old Testament approach to relationships
  1. It forbids wrong action against a brother
  2. It forbids adding to a brother's burdens

III. The Significance

A. The application to today
  1. Internal opposition is not uncommon when God begins to work
  2. Look beyond to the New Testament for the way to treat a brother
B. God places a high premium on "one another" in the New Testament
  1. There are more than three dozen references, and all are commandments
  2. There are more than two dozen things we are commanded to do or to refrain from doing

Conclusion:

How are you treating your brother? What are you doing for one another? What will you do for one another?

Some People Will Stop at Nothing
Nehemiah 6

Introduction:

We say, "Some people will stop at nothing," and by that we mean that some are pushy and determined, others are stubborn and self-willed, and still others want what they want so badly they won't allow anything to thwart them from securing it. When it comes to people who will stop at nothing, however, Satan is the ultimate example.

I. **Satan Will Stop at Nothing to Keep You from Serving God and from Doing His Will**
    A. He will use every means at his disposal:
        1. Diversion—"Let's talk about it" (v. 2)
        2. Lies and innuendoes (vv. 5–7)
        3. Appeals to compromise (v. 10)
        4. Open threats (v. 19)
    B. He will keep trying even when thwarted (vv. 4, 19)
    C. He will use anyone or anything available
    D. He will suit his attack to your personality and situation

II. **You Can Stop Satan When He Will Stop at Nothing**
    A. Notice Nehemiah's response
        1. Be ready for his attacks—they come when progress is being made, and they come after achievement
        2. Refuse to reason about what you know to be God's will (v. 3)
        3. Determine to face continuing attacks in the same way—if something was true at the start, it is still true (v. 4)
        4. Be sure your motives and actions are pure—the best answer to his challenge is a life without blame (v. 8)
        5. Refute false charges openly—especially when they deal with morals, financial integrity, or doctrinal purity (v. 8)
        6. Pray for strength in time of need—this undergirds all that Nehemiah did in this situation (v. 9)
        7. Keep courage in the bad times—"don't doubt in the dark what God has given you in the light" (vv. 11–13)
        8. Resolve to do nothing that shows compromise or weakness (vv. 11–13)

9. Turn those whom Satan uses over to God—let God take care of settling the scores of life (v. 14)
10. Always recognize the role Satan plays in these attacks—he is behind every attempt to keep you from obeying and serving the Lord (v. 18)

B. Even when Satan will stop at nothing, you can defeat him by responding in the same way as Nehemiah

III. God Is Specially Honored When We Stop Satan When He Will Stop at Nothing

A. When the enemy has thrown his best and you are unmoved, it is obviously of God
B. Those who have allowed themselves to be used of Satan are obviously diminished when they are not able to stop you
C. God will not normally stop Satan, but He has given you what you need to do so, if you will

Conclusion:

Have you run into major opposition or trouble? If so, Satan is behind it as he will stop at nothing to keep you from obeying and serving the Lord. Satan can be stopped when he will stop at nothing, but only you can stop him.

Revive Us Again

Nehemiah 8:1–13

Introduction:

You can't schedule a revival, but you can have a revival whenever you choose. An individual can have spiritual renewal any time, and if enough individuals do so at one time, an entire church can be revived.

I. **You Probably Need Revival Right Now**
   A. "But I am one of God's people"
      1. The Jews in Nehemiah's day were certainly God's people
      2. They were in need of revival
   B. "But I am actively involved in His work"
      1. The Jews were actively involved in His work
      2. Actually, their involvement may have created greater need for revival
   C. "But I have just had a notable spiritual achievement"
      1. The Jews had just had notable achievement
      2. The need for revival actually may be greatest right after a victory

II. **The Revival You Need**
   A. It involves a renewed emphasis on the Word of God (vv. 1–3)
      1. All Scriptural revivals are based on the Word of God
      2. It involves understanding the meaning (application) of the Word (v. 7)
   B. It produces certain effects
      1. A recognition of personal spiritual need—they wept (v. 9b)
      2. A sense of great joy and rejoicing—any time facing your sin does not result in joy, there is something wrong (v. 12)
      3. A renewal of spiritual interest—genuine revival always leaves one more interested in the things of the Lord
   C. It always exalts the Lord—the people stood out of reverence for the Word (vv. 5–6)

III. How You Can Know Genuine Revival
    A. Admit the need in your life
        1. If you have ever been closer to the Lord than now
        2. If the Word of God has become routine in your life
    B. Turn to the Word of God
        1. Take time to expose yourself to it
        2. Pray that God will use it in your life
    C. Respond to what God shows you through the Word
        1. Confess sin
        2. Make commitments
    D. Seek in every possible way to exalt the Lord

Conclusion:

You probably need revival right now. Will you return to the Word of God with an open heart? Will you allow the Word of God to work in you? Will you seek revival?

"Come On, Get Happy!"

Nehemiah 8:1–13

Introduction:

"No language has as many words for joy and rejoicing as the Hebrew." Joy is something not to be lightly dismissed.

I. **A Matter of Context**
   A. The wall-building project was completed
   B. Nehemiah had ordered that the Word of God be read and preached
   C. The people were overcome by a realization of their sin
   D. The people began to show their sorrow
   E. Nehemiah recognized the limits even of godly sorrow
      1. This all happened on a feast day
      2. He ordered the people to stop sorrowing and to get happy

II. **A Matter of Commandment**
   A. This was not optional
      1. There is no excuse or rationalization for the absence of joy
      2. It must have been possible for them to "get happy" if they were commanded to do so
   B. This is not the only time this happens in the Word

III. **A Matter of Change**
   A. Change comes through changing our thinking
   B. Change comes through changing our actions

IV. **A Matter of Choice—Some people have no joy because**
   A. They are chronically unhappy
   B. They have an agenda of their own
   C. They have a problem with sin

V. **A Matter of Concern**
   A. Joy is part of God's character (Ps. 104:31)
   B. Joy is part of God's purposes (Phil. 4:4)

VI. **A Matter of Celebration—We rejoice in**
   A. Our forgiveness (Ps. 51:8, 12)
   B. Our relationship (Ps. 28:7)
   C. His presence and indwelling (Ps. 16:11)
   D. Our assurance (Rom. 15:13)
   E. Our eternal expectation (Jude 1:24)

VII. A Matter of Consequences: "The joy of the Lord is your strength"
A. It is our strength in trouble
B. It is our strength in testing
C. It is our strength in temptation
D. It is our strength in tedium

Conclusion:
These people were rebuked for being sorrowful for sin and they were told, "Come on, get happy!" How much more are we blameworthy if we are without joy for any other reasons?

Job: Real Life Experiences

Introduction:
"What causes a person to suffer is one of the surest indications of what it is that he or she believes."

I. **The Story of Job**
   A. The testing of Job (1:1–2:13)—we are dealing with a very good man (note what upsets him)
   B. The trial of Job (3:1–37:24)—his friends provide further trial because each in his own way completely misunderstands
   C. The truth for Job (38:1–41:34)—the main question to Job—"Who are you?"
   D. The triumph of Job (42:1–17)—everything restored to him, but his greatest triumph is in self-revelation

II. **The Lessons from Job**
   A. Beware of oversimplification (John 9:2)
      1. "Trials and prosperity are the result of sin or obedience"
      2. This was the message of Job's friends, and it is not so
   B. Give the Devil his due (1 Peter 5:8)
      1. He has incredible power—look what he did to Job
      2. He was limited to what God allowed—this is a great assurance in trial
   C. Let God be God (Isa. 55:8–9)
      1. We do not fully understand every aspect of the story
      2. One of the main points of the story is that we can't understand God
   D. Come, give glory to the Lord (Ps. 103:19–22)
      1. The glory of the Lord is the ultimate issue
      2. Sometimes it requires suffering to glorify the Lord
   E. To err is human (1 John 1:8–10; James 3:2)
      1. Job's friends and Elihu were all completely wrong
      2. Job was wrong in much of what he said as he showed his humanity; but God remembers what we forget (Ps. 103:14)
   F. It's all for the best (Rom. 8:28)
      1. God was working out His purposes through it all (the more intense your suffering, the more likely the Lord knows everything about it)
      2. Job came out better than he had been (this will be true of believers also—but the restitution may come later)

G. Misery loves company (2 Cor. 1:3–6)
   1. Millions have been helped by Job's experiences
   2. Job's response to God's dealings has become Job's gift to the human race—even as our responses can become the same thing to those around us
H. The last straw (1 Cor. 10:13)
   1. "God knew Job's spiritual condition and would not have entrusted him with such tragedies if there had been doubt of the outcome"
   2. Your trials may take you right to the edge, but they will not take you over the edge!

III. The Challenges of Job
A. My personal perspective
   1. There is a need to review these truths continually
   2. There is a need to see trials as "gifts" carefully chosen by a loving Father to produce responses in me that will glorify Him
B. My personal performance
   1. There is a need to be thankful
   2. There is a need to get busy
   3. There is a need to remember all the things I have promised God

Conclusion:
   "As Christians, we would do well to ask ourselves what sort of things we complain about, and what causes us the greatest pain and fear."

Flashes of Light in the Darkest Night

Job 19:21–28

Introduction:

The question of Job: Will a man serve God for nothing? The answer of Job: Yes, but with great difficulty!

I. **Look at Job**
    A. The Prologue: the story of Job (Job 1:1–2:8)
    B. The Dialogue: the struggles of Job (2:9–27:34)
    C. The Apologue: the sequel of Job (38:1–42:17)

II. **Listen to Job**
    A. Job struggles:
        1. With his circumstances
        2. With himself—this is a big factor in the book
        3. With his wife
        4. With his friends—they said the right things to the wrong person, the wrong things to the right person, the wrong things to the wrong person, but never the right things to the right person
        5. With his God
    B. Job speaks
        1. He reveals a glimpse of a personal redemption—note the personal pronouns
        2. He reveals a glimpse of an eternal resurrection—"He shall stand upon the earth"—"In my flesh I shall see God"
        3. He reveals a glimpse of a supernatural recognition—"Whom I shall see for myself and mine eyes shall behold"—even though I feel like I am being destroyed at the present moment

III. **Learn from Job**
    A. Lesson #1: God always has His purposes
        1. His purpose here? To glorify Himself through His servant
        2. Remember that this purpose was unknown to Job
    B. Lesson #2: It is natural for man to struggle
        1. We get some unrealistic teaching in this area
        2. God rebukes Job on this, but the rebuke is very gentle
    C. Lesson #3: It is proper to share our struggles with God
        1. We should only complain to One who can do something about our complaint

2. This is not only an Old Testament view, as Paul struggled with God over his thorn in the flesh and came to peace only when he was assured that nothing would be done about the problem

D. Lesson #4: Great flashes often come in greatest darkness
   1. Job may well be the earliest book in the Bible
   2. On that basis, his spiritual development is incredible

E. Lesson #5: The lessons are always worth the struggle
   1. Look at what Job learned
   2. We say, "How can I get out of this?" when we should be saying, "What can I get out of this?"

F. Lesson #6: Ultimately, things always turn out right
   1. Note the word "ultimately"
   2. Many, if not most, things turn out right on earth, but all will turn out right in heaven

G. Lesson #7: The main message of Job: "Hang on to your faith"
   1. Job is a book of broad perspective
   2. We see much that Job never saw, but we would say to Job what He says to us, "Hang in there!"

Conclusion:

Are you living in the book of Job? Then learn the lesson of Job.

Taste and See!

Psalm 34:8

Introduction:

We can get too much of a good thing in many areas, but there is at least one area in which we can never get enough.

I. **The Centerpiece: "The Lord is good"**
   A. He is good in His character (Matt. 19:17)
   B. He is good in His gifts (James 1:17)
   C. He is good in His withholdings (Ps. 84:11)
   D. He is good in His allowances (James 1:2–5)

II. **The Challenge: "Taste and see"**
   A. The meaning
      1. "Taste"—discern the identity of food—examine it thoroughly
      2. Put the matter to the test of experience by exploring what He has provided
   B. The manner
      1. By using what He has given
      2. By resting on His promises in trials
      3. By exploring His potentialities
      4. By withholding judgment on His dealings

III. **The Conclusion: "Blessed is the man that trusteth in Him"**
   A. "Trust"—believing facts enough to act on them
   B. There are two applications
      1. Believe the facts of the Bible enough to obey the will of God
      2. Believe the facts of salvation enough to trust the Lord
   C. The aim of the Bible is to produce a supernatural experience
      1. Have you had one?
      2. Are you having a continuing one?

Conclusion:

The banquet table is spread. Will you taste and see? It is the only way you can know!

Don't Bother God?

Psalm 50:15

Introduction:
Have you ever felt awkward about going to God in a time of trouble? He wants you to come because He is honored by it. He actually commands it!

I. **A Commandment: "Call upon me in the day of trouble"**
    A. "In the day of trouble"
        1. Every day is a day of trouble
        2. This, however, refers to time of special trouble
    B. He wants us to call upon him because it involves
        1. Recognition of our God
        2. Experience of our God
        3. Exaltation of our God
        4. Submission to our God
        5. Confidence in our God

II. **A Commitment: "I will deliver thee"**
    A. It is a practical deliverance
        1. There is solid, substantial aid—"I"
        2. It is either from, out of, or through
    B. It is a positive deliverance—leave the "how" with the God who said He will do it
    C. It is a punctual deliverance—leave the "when" with God as troubles always have an appointed end
    D. It is a personal deliverance—"The Lord God Himself, He will do it for you."
    E. It is a permanent deliverance—you will be back into trouble again, but the promise is never used up

III. **A Context (v. 14)**
    A. The near context—a promise best claimed when
        1. You are walking with the Lord
        2. You are keeping your spiritual commitments
    B. The far context—it goes back to verse 8
        1. God doesn't want our offerings
        2. He wants our praise, vow keeping, and cries

IV. **A Consequence: "And thou shalt glorify me"**
    A. It is strange that we should glorify God through troubles
    B. The ways in which it is done

1. By gratitude of heart
2. By a testimony in word to His faithfulness
3. By growth in faith
4. By an increase in patience to wait on Him
5. By living to His praise

Conclusion:

Are you in a time of trouble? Call upon God and He will deliver you. Have you been delivered? Then glorify the Lord.

How to Bear Your Own Burdens

Psalm 55:22

Introduction:

We are told to bear our own burdens, but sometimes that is a very difficult assignment. The psalmist shows us how to do so successfully.

I. **Our Temptation in Trial**
  A. Complaint
   1. David fell into this trap (v. 2)
   2. The usual complaint? God is dealing harshly with me
   3. The alternative? "Shall we receive good at the hand of God, and shall we not receive evil?"
  B. Despair
   1. David fell into this also (vv. 4–5)
   2. There is never a cause for the child of God to despair
   3. You may have come to the end of your poor strength, but you haven't come to the end of God's mercy
  C. Flight
   1. David turned to this also (vv. 6–8)
   2. Fleeing from problems seldom solves them
   3. We are likely to get into greater trouble by fleeing than by standing
  D. Vengeful thinking and acting
   1. David fell into this trap also (v. 9)
   2. We are ourselves injured when we desire injury to our foes
   3. Not only should we not speak harshly, we should not even think harshly of our enemies

II. **Our Commandment in Confusion**
  A. We must trace the source of the burden
   1. Everything that comes to us has either been sent or allowed by God
   2. We must look to the Lord as the ultimate cause
  B. We must tell the Lord about it
   1. Talk with Him first about all the affairs of life
   2. Tell the Lord what you are experiencing and how you feel about it

C. We must patiently wait its removal
   1. If it has come from Him, it can only be removed by Him
   2. When its purpose is fulfilled, it will be removed
D. We must believe that it will work out to our good—if God has allowed it, it must be to a good purpose or He wouldn't have allowed it at all
E. We must leave the burden with the Lord
   1. It is foolish to roll a burden on Him and then carry it also
   2. If the burden really is cast, the heart should be unburdened and the soul at rest
F. We must continue to communicate with ourselves
   1. Every time the burden resurfaces, talk with yourself about it
   2. Argue with yourself about the burden—give yourself reasons not to bear it again

III. Our Assurance in Anxiety
A. Sustenance—"He shall sustain thee"
   1. The idea in the word is to feed or nourish
   2. It does not indicate removal of the burden—rather it indicates that He will bear it and will feed and nourish us
B. Sufferance—"He shall never suffer the righteous to be moved"
   1. He will never allow us to bear a burden heavier than we can bear
   2. At the appropriate time, God will play the good father

Conclusion:

We all have burdens to carry and there is a message here for each. Why will you carry the load when someone else offers to help you.

Unto Thee, O Lord

Psalm 86

Introduction:

Do you ever tangle with the "d" words: *down, disturbed, defeated, despairing, depressed, distressed, deflated, dejected, dismayed, deserted, desolate, distracted, discouraged, dishonored, dissatisfied?* David surely did, but he found the answer to all of them.

I. **His Complaint (vv. 1–4,14)**
   A. We don't know the setting for sure, but David is very involved with "d" words
      1. This may have been during time of fleeing from Saul
      2. This may have also been at the time of Absalom's rebellion
   B. Note
      1. "I am poor and needy"—I am down on myself
      2. "I am holy"—I am among those special to you
      3. "I keep crying to you daily"—I am faithful in prayer
      4. "I lift up my soul"—I am taking strong spiritual action

II. **His Conduct (vv. 6, 16–17)**
   A. David's immediate reaction was to turn to the Lord
      1. He brought both prayer and supplications (v. 6)
      2. He asked for God to "turn" to him—look upon him (v. 16)
      3. He asked God to help him as a token or to give him some indication that God was for him and still on his side (v. 17)
   B. David showed thoughtful intelligence
      1. The place to turn in the time of need was to the Lord
      2. David did so as a regular habit

III. **His Confidence (vv. 7b, 13)**
   A. He turned to the Lord because of his confidence that God would answer—there is not much sense in turning to the Lord if one is not sure of an answer (v. 7b)
   B. He based his confidence on God's previous performance—every deliverance ought to make us trust Him more (v. 17b)

IV. His Comprehension

    A. David turned to a God worth turning to

        1. There is nothing vague in his faith

        2. There is nothing casual in his understanding

    B. The things David knew about the God to whom he turned

        1. God is good—whatever defines good is resident in Him (v. 5)

        2. God is ready to forgive—this almost has the idea that He is anxious for an opportunity (v. 5)

        3. God is plenteous in mercy—the NIV says, "abounding in love" (v. 5)

        4. There is none like God—among all those who claim to be gods, there is no god like God (vv. 8, 10)

        5. There are no works like His works—no one can "do marvelous deeds" like God (vv. 8, 10)

        6. God is great—this can be applied to virtually every adjective describing Him (v. 10)

        7. God's mercy is great—there is a difference between mercy and grace (v. 13)

        8. God is full of compassion—He is compassionate to the greatest degree (v. 15)

        9. God is gracious—grace is so much a part of His character that it becomes a description (v. 15)

        10. God is long-suffering—"Slow to anger" (v. 15)

        11. God is plenteous in truth—absolutely faithful (v. 15)

V. David's Commitment (vv. 7, 11–12)

    A. He made three commitments

        1. "I will call upon thee"

        2. "I will walk in thy truth"

        3. "I will praise thee"

    B. His commitments were not conditional

        1. He said he would do these things regardless

        2. These things are right whether or not any answers come

Conclusion:

David tangled with the "d" words, but he found the answer. The answer was in God.

Know Ye and Do Ye

Psalm 100

Introduction:

The old town crier said, "Hear Ye! Hear Ye! Hear Ye!" He then said what it was that he wanted you to hear. The psalmist in Psalm 100:3 says, "Know Ye!" He then tells us what it is he wants us to know.

I. Know Ye

A. His Godhead—"the Lord He is God"
   1. This is a continuing theme in the Old Testament
   2. This is dramatically demonstrated in the contest with Pharaoh and in the giving of the law
   3. This has practical meaning—there is no other God, and all ways do not lead to God

B. His prerogatives of creation—"It is He that hath made us and not we ourselves"
   1. This is a constant assertion in Scripture (Acts 17:24)
   2. He has made us—this is twice true in regard to the Christian
   3. This has practical meaning—we must accept our unchangeable aspects and also accept His absolute sovereignty

C. His care—"We are His people and the sheep of His pasture"
   1. We belong to Him—both by creation and by redemption
   2. We enjoy His special care—"sheep of His pasture"
   3. This has practical meaning—His care is as extensive as that of a shepherd, and we are never out of that care

D. His character (v. 5)
   1. This verse selects prominent traits in God (not what we often focus on)
   2. Note three characteristics
      a. Goodness—general word for all that is good
      b. Mercy—an aspect of goodness—not getting what is deserved
      c. Truth—absolute self-consistency
   3. This has practical meaning—it describes the God with whom we have to deal, and it takes away all terror in our relationship with Him

II. **Do Ye—we aren't left with a stack of information but rather with an application of truth**
   A. Worship Him (vv. 1, 4)
      1. Focus on praise and thanksgiving
      2. If God is what we are told He is, then He is worthy of praise
      3. To know Him without worshipping Him is to miss the point
   B. Serve Him (v. 2)
      1. There is an element of servanthood, voluntary slavery in it
      2. The emphasis is on joy, mirth, gladness
      3. To know Him without gladly serving Him misses the point

Conclusion:

There are four things the psalmist wants us to know about God: 1) that He, indeed and alone, is God; 2) that He created us with all that implies; 3) that He cares for us; and 4) that His character is ultimately good.

The Lord Is Merciful

Psalm 103:8–12, 17–18

Introduction:
"The Lord is merciful and gracious." We want to concentrate on God's mercy here.

I. **God Has Mercy Adequate for All Needs**
    A. "Plenteous in mercy" (v. 8)
        1. This means abundant, overflowing
        2. This contrasts with verse 6—God is more likely to show mercy than He is to practice judgment
    B. Note the comparison (v. 11)
        1. The heaven/earth comparison is designed to express infinity
        2. God's mercy is indescribable, incomprehensible
    C. Note the expression—were it not for
        1. Sparing mercy, we would all go to hell
        2. Inviting mercy, none would ever hear the Gospel
        3. Saving mercy, no sinner's prayer would every be answered
        4. Upholding mercy, none would be able to live the Christian life
        5. Consoling mercy, all would be swallowed up by grief
        6. Infinite mercy, all would be cut off from the earth
        7. Everlasting mercy, none would ever get to heaven

II. **God Shows His Mercy in Many Ways**
    A. In regard to His anger
        1. He is "slow to anger"—extremely patient and long-suffering (v. 8)
        2. "He will not always chide"—He does not jump on every violation (v. 9)
        3. "Neither will He keep His anger forever"—God holds no grudges (vv. 8–9)
    B. In regard to our sins
        1. "He hath not dealt with us after our sins"—He can't deal with our sins because He has already dealt with them in Christ (v. 10)
        2. "Nor rewarded us according to our iniquities"—beware of an overly judgmental view of God (v. 10)

3. "As far as the east is from the west . . ."—This is obviously meant to be a figure of speech for infinity (v. 12)

III. God's Mercy Calls Forth a Response
    A. ". . . his mercy toward them that fear Him" (v. 11)
        1. All men know something of His mercy
        2. The mercy described here is primarily for His people
    B. "The mercy of the Lord is from everlasting. . . ." (v. 17)
        1. His mercy transcends time as well as space
        2. It is conditional—"Upon them that fear Him"
    C. It is conditional even among those that love Him (v. 18)
        1. It is to those who live within His covenant
        2. It is to those who keep His commandments

Conclusion:

There is more of God's mercy than all that has been used. God's mercy challenges us. It is most bestowed where there is most wrong. It is most beneficial where there is obedience.

Thanksgiving and Goodness
Psalm 106:1

Introduction:
The Bible repeatedly links praise and thanksgiving with the goodness of God. That relationship can be explained by the answers to three questions.

I. **Why Should We Be Thankful?**
   A. Because of defined good
      1. Ultimately, whatever we know of good comes from knowing God
      2. What is good? Tell me about God
   B. Because of considered good
      1. He is good in His character—all His attributes
      2. He is good in His thoughts
      3. He is good in His words
      4. He is good in His acts
   C. Because of unique good
      1. God is absolutely good
      2. None but God is good

II. **For What Should We Be Thankful?**
   A. Things withheld by the Lord
      1. If He is good, then His withholding must be good
      2. We should praise rather than complain
   B. Things sent from the Lord
      1. If He is good, then whatever He sends us must be good
      2. We should praise rather than resist
   C. Things allowed by the Lord
      1. If He is good, then whatever He allows must be good
      2. We should praise rather than question
   D. Things in response to disobeying the Lord
      1. Some things in our lives we bring on ourselves
      2. We should praise Him that He chastises us to get our attention

III. **How Should We Be Thankful?**
   A. In attitude
      1. Gratitude is first an attitude
      2. We need a thankful spirit—one that deliberately focuses on finding causes for praise and thanksgiving

B. In word
    1. We should be constant in our expression of praise
    2. We should be looking for opportunities to praise
C. In action
    1. Praise and gratitude should show themselves
    2. What are tangible ways in which praise can be shown?

Conclusion:

The goodness of God should lead us to repentance. The goodness of God should motivate us to obedience. The goodness of God should move us to thanksgiving.

Practical Pointers for Positive Christianity

Proverbs 3

Introduction:
The Bible is an intensely practical book designed to direct our living. We should never be satisfied with Bible knowledge; we should develop Bible practice.

I. **The Principle of Obedience (v. 1)**
   A. "Don't let my law get out of your mind"
   B. "Let thine heart keep"—the precepts of the Word are designed to be kept
   C. They have a reward (v. 2)

II. **The Principle of Balance (v. 3)**
   A. Both mercy (love, pity, compassion) and truth (integrity, judgment) are necessary
   B. You must possess them inwardly and outwardly
   C. This is a difficult mix of virtues
   D. They also have a reward (v. 4)

III. **The Principle of Trust (v. 5)**
   A. "Trust in the Lord" defines the object
   B. "With all thine heart" describes the manner
   C. "Lean not to thine own understanding" provides the caution
   D. "In all thy ways acknowledge Him" prescribes the solution
   E. "He shall direct thy paths" indicates the promise

IV. **The Principle of Practical Humility (v. 7)**
   A. "Be not wise in thine own eyes" has to do with one's own estimation of one's self
   B. How to do it?
      1. "Fear the Lord"—give Him proper estimation
      2. "Depart from evil"—stay away from trouble
   C. It also has its reward (v. 8)

V. **The Principle of Giving (v. 9)**
   A. This is broader than any tithe commandment
   B. This involves honoring the Lord
   C. A reward is promised—but that is not the best motive (v. 10)

VI. The Principle of Submission (v. 11)
A. "Despise not" (reject, condemn as unworthy) and "weary" (loathe, throw up, get sick of)
B. The "chastening"—disciplines of the Lord
C. God has reasons for discipline:
1. To rebuke backsliding
2. To recall from wandering
3. To arouse us from lethargy
4. To alert us to spiritual dullness
5. To advance us to a higher spiritual state

VII. The Principle of Judgment (v. 21)
A. "Sound wisdom" (basic life principles) and "discretion" (ability to see the difference between)
B. Both characteristics are found in the Word of God
C. The Bible enables us to make wise right or wrong decisions in life

VIII. The Principle of Responsibility (v. 27)
A. The principle: "Withhold not good"
B. The principle conditioned:
1. "From those to whom it is due"
2. "When it is in the power of your hand to do it"
C. The principle illustrated (v. 28)

IX. The Principle of Relationships (vv. 29–30)
A. "Devise not evil . . ."—Don't be a troublemaker by abusing any confidence placed in you
B. "Strive not without a cause"—Don't be the one to start the fight without a very good cause

X. The Principle of Contentment (v. 31)
A. "Envy not"—Do not covet or desire to have
B. "Choose none of his ways"—Do not copy what he does
C. Reasons are given for not doing so (v. 32)

Conclusion:
THE BIBLE: not just a book of facts to be learned and known, but a book of principles to be practiced in everyday life.

The Ultimate Difference

Isaiah 55:8–9

Introduction:
Some things are so very obvious, and this passage speaks of
one of them. Even though this truth is obvious, however, there
is still much for us to learn about it.

I. **God Is Different from Us**
   A. This is an obvious fact—we can't conceive of greater
      differences
   B. Here are sample differences
      1. He is concerned with our comfort; we are not even
         concerned with His honor
      2. He considers our interests; we are not concerned
         with His glory
      3. He watches over our safety; we don't bother to keep
         His commandments
      4. He loads us with benefits; we load Him with our
         sins
      5. He gives us all we have; we bring Him little thanks
         in return

II. **God Is Infinitely Above Us**
   A. Here are sample areas
      1. We are selfish; God is beneficent
      2. We are vindictive; God is magnanimous
      3. We think crookedly; God thinks uprightly
      4. We think on the lowest levels; God thinks sublimely
      5. We operate finitely; God operates infinitely
      6. We think erroneously; God thinks infallibly
   B. Here are some things true of God
      1. His ways are ways of holiness and purity
      2. His ways are ways of tenderness and love
      3. His ways are ways of truth
      4. His ways are ways of forgiveness and peace

III. **God Relates to Us Through These Differences**
   A. We simply can't expect to understand God—God, if
      He is to be God, must be beyond understanding
   B. We can't quarrel with God's operations or working—it
      is pointless to enter into controversy with God
   C. We can expect God to do things well beyond our
      anticipations and imaginations

D. We should develop an understanding of sovereignty and surrender—He is absolutely sovereign, and we are at our best when we completely surrender to His will

E. This all makes pardon and mercy possible even though incomprehensible—what we can't conceive, He can accomplish

Conclusion:

God is different from us. God is infinitely above us. God ministers to us through the differences.

The Smile of God
Isaiah 66:1–2

Introduction:
They had built God a lovely temple, but He wasn't as interested in the temple as He was in the lives of certain of His people. He singled out three groups for His special attention: the poor, the contrite, and the group we are most interested in, the ones that tremble at His Word.

I. **The Meaning: Who are those who tremble at His Word?**
   A. Who they are not
      1. They are not proud people
      2. They are not profane people—people who would mock at sin or at God's Word
      3. They are not perfunctory people—people just going through the motions
      4. They are not patronizing people—people who sit in judgment on the Word
      5. They are not presumptuous people
   B. Who they are
      1. They are people who believe there is a Word from God
         a. They believe that the Bible is different from all other sacred books
         b. They believe that the reason this is true is because the Bible is a word from God
      2. They are people who are acquainted with God's Word
         a. One can't tremble without hearing and reading it
         b. The more we understand it, the more it will cause us to fear

II. **The Reasons: Why do they tremble at His Word?**
   A. Because of His exceeding majesty
      1. Those who saw even His reflected majesty trembled
      2. The Word of God reflects the majesty of God
   B. Because of its searching power
      1. We should pray Hebrews 4:12 into our lives
      2. The Word has the ability to show us what we are
   C. Because of its threatening demeanor
      1. It threatens judgment to the sinner
      2. It threatens recompense to the Saint
   D. Because of the fear of breaking God's law

      1. There should be no desire to offend such a loving Father
      2. There should be no desire to go beyond His established perimeters
   E. Because of the weakness of the human state
      1. We all know of our tendency to "miss the mark"
      2. We should never be confident in ourselves

III. The Result: How does God view those who tremble at His Word?
   A. He will look to them with attention
   B. He will look to them with approbation
   C. He will look to them with acceptance
   D. He will look to them with affection
   E. He will look to them with approval

Conclusion:

Should there be fear in the Christian life? First Peter 1:17 speaks of the fear that is in view here: Will you tremble at the Word so that God can look to you?

Show and Tell

Jeremiah 33:3

Introduction:

Do you ever get frustrated with the Christian life? Do you ever get frustrated in prayer? Then Jeremiah has something for you.

I. **The Situation of Jeremiah**
   A. He was in confining circumstances (32:1–5)
      1. "If you don't like the message, kill the messenger"
      2. He was thrown in prison for telling the truth
   B. He was receiving confusing communications (32:6–15)
      1. Conditions were awful in Jerusalem—Babylon was at the gates, and the city was being dismantled to shore up the walls—collapse and captivity were sure
      2. He was directed to purchase a field—humanly speaking, it was a foolish move, but it was designed by God to communicate some truth
   C. He was drawing conflicting conclusions
      1. The nation was about to be conquered but a new purchase was to be made—what does this mean?
      2. He brings his confusion to the Lord (32:16–25)
      3. God gives him a partial answer (32:26–44)

II. **The Invitation to Jeremiah**
   A. A general expression—"Call unto me"
      1. In this and every other time of trial
      2. Do so more often
   B. A gracious guarantee—"I will answer thee"
      1. This is a clear promise
      2. This pertains to everyone
   C. A generous provision—"I will tell you great and hidden, unsearchable things that you do not know"
      1. This part of the promise was specific to Jeremiah
      2. God promises to give information for his confusion—"Call to me; I will answer you and tell you things that you do not know but that you need to know"

III. **The Application from Jeremiah**
   A. Here is a specific promise
      1. It is given to Jeremiah to ease his confusion
      2. It is tailored to his specific situation
      3. God says, "I will tell you what you need to know"

B. Here is an expanding potential
 1. God is expressing here that He will give what is needed in response to prayer
 2. Thus, "In every situation call to me, and I will answer and will meet your need"
 3. Taking the promise in its context really makes it more practical
C. Here is a tailored provision
 1. Are you frustrated? Call to God! He will hear and give you what you need in response to your prayer
 2. You may not know what you need to know; He does
 3. God gave a word to Jeremiah; we already have a Word from God—your answer may lie in what God has already said in the narrative and biographical portions of Scripture

Conclusion:

Jeremiah was in bad circumstances, with conflicting information, and totally confused. God said, "Call to me, I'll answer with what you need." Are you frustrated, confused by circumstances or unanswered prayer? God says, "Call to me, I'll answer with what you need." We need to be reminded that God sees a bigger picture than any we see.

A Powerful Promise

Jeremiah 33:3

Introduction:

Many times we seize God's promises without considering the context in which they were given. We always lose something when we do that, and this is a case in point.

I. **The Setting of the Promise**
    A. Trace Israel's history from the death of Solomon
    B. The Northern Kingdom was already lost
    C. The Southern Kingdom was about to be lost
    D. Zedekiah was king, and he was one of the last kings of Judah
    E. The city was under siege by Nebuchadnezzar of Babylon

II. **The One to Whom the Promise Was Given**
    A. Jeremiah, the "weeping prophet"
    B. He had been predicting gloom and doom for the nation
        1. He told of Babylon's coming
        2. He recommended surrender to Nebuchadnezzar
        3. He had been imprisoned by Zedekiah for his trouble
    C. He now gives a new message
        1. He predicts a return from captivity
        2. He predicts a future kingdom
    D. He is told to buy a field in land that was then occupied by Babylon
        1. This is a sign from the Lord concerning his prophecy
        2. This is designed to impress people
    E. He is a very confused prophet
        1. He has been told to predict gloom and doom
        2. He is now told to tell of cheer and hope
        3. He is told to confirm his prediction with a symbolic purchase

III. **The Giver of the Promise**
    A. The Lord God of Israel (30:2)
    B. The One who said, "I am the Lord" (32:27)
    C. The Lord for whom nothing is too difficult (32:27)
    D. The Lord, the Creator and Orderer (33:2)

IV. **The Promise Itself**
    A. "Call to me"
    B. "I will answer you"

C. "I will show you"
D. "Great and mighty" (hidden, unsearchable) things
E. "Which thou knowest not"—which is what is causing your confusion

V. The Implications of the Promise
A. Some were specific to Jeremiah
   1. Are you confused by what is going on?
   2. Call to me—I'll help you in your confusion
B. Some are general for all
C. Some are particular
   1. Are you going through a time of trial as Jeremiah did, are you confused about what is going on in your life, or are you faced with a difficult command?
   2. Call to me, in prayer, and I will show great and unsearchable things you don't know

Conclusion:
We live in turbulent times—especially in individual lives. Call to Him and He will answer. His answer will include great and unsearchable things that you could know in no other way.

I Hereby Resolve . . .

Daniel 1:8

Introduction:
Daniel is unique in the Bible in that nothing negative is said
about him. He had a long and extraordinary life, and it was
very eventful.

I. **An Examination of Daniel**
    A. Personal
        1. He was a Jew taken captive to Babylon
        2. He was very young at the time (vv. 15–17)
        3. He was added to the royal court while in captivity
        4. His name was changed, indicating an attempt to
           change his religion
    B. Vocational
        1. He started out as a "wise man"
        2. He was elevated to high office—administrator
           (2:46–49)
        3. He was made supervisor over the supervisors (6:1–3)
        4. He served successfully through one change of
           government and through three administrations
           (Nebuchadnezzar, Belshazzar, Darius, Cyrus)

II. **The Exploits of Daniel**
    A. His accomplishments
        1. The interpretation of Nebuchadnezzar's vision
           (chap. 2)
        2. The interpretation of Nebuchadnezzar's dream
           (chap. 4)
        3. The reading of the writing on the wall (chap. 5)
        4. The reception of visions (chap. 7ff.)
    B. His refusals
        1. To eat the meat provided for him by the king—this
           jeopardized his advancement in the court (1:8–16)
        2. To alter his personal religious observance—this
           actually jeopardized his life (6:4–10)

III. **The Explanation of Daniel—how could he do these
things?**
    A. "Daniel purposed"
        1. "Daniel resolved" (NIV)
        2. This was a specific decision of the will

B. "Daniel purposed in his heart"
1. His decision was made on the deepest internal level
2. His decision was made in advance

IV. The Example of Daniel
A. He shows us the value of resolution
1. We must always view making resolutions with caution
2. But we rarely do wrong when we have decided ahead of time that we will not do so
B. The direction of his resolution
1. Daniel had decided what he would not do
2. There is also a place for decisions regarding what one will do

Conclusion:

Daniel purposed in his heart, and as a result, he did not sin. What purpose do you need to make in your heart?